The Three Chicks

Trilogy Christian Publishers
A Wholly Owned Subsidiary of Trinity Broadcasting Network
2442 Michelle Drive
Tustin, CA 92780

Copyright © 2023 by Kimberly Boyer

All rights reserved, including the right to reproduce this book or portions thereof in any form whatsoever.

For information, address Trilogy Christian Publishing
Rights Department, 2442 Michelle Drive, Tustin, Ca 92780.
Trilogy Christian Publishing/ TBN and colophon are trademarks of Trinity Broadcasting Network.

For information about special discounts for bulk purchases, please contact Trilogy Christian Publishing.

Manufactured in the United States of America

Trilogy Disclaimer: The views and content expressed in this book are those of the author and may not necessarily reflect the views and doctrine of Trilogy Christian Publishing or the Trinity Broadcasting Network.

10 9 8 7 6 5 4 3 2 1

Library of Congress Cataloging-in-Publication Data is available.

ISBN 979-8-88738-798-7 (Print Book)
ISBN 979-8-88738-799-4 (ebook)

The Three Chicks

Kimberly Boyer

There once was a Mama Chick who had three little chicks: Kelsey, Keisha, and Zeta.

She loved her little chickens so very much. She thought of each one of them every day. She wondered what she could do for each one to make them feel special.

She always made sure they had plenty of chicken feed and water. She made sure to wash their feathers every day and combed them with a special feather comb.

When the weather was warm, they would all get together to have a toenail-painting party. They would listen to music, paint toenails, and drink soda. They had fun just hanging out.

Every Sunday, Mama Chick would take her baby chicks to church to worship God and give thanks. Mama was very thankful that God trusted her to raise these chicks. Mama always tried to teach her chicks to love.

Mama loved her chicks very much. Mama also loved Papa Rooster. Papa had always been there for Mama whenever she needed him.

They all lived in the barnyard with their friends.

In the evenings they all went to roost, and the Lord watched over them as they slept.

The End

Printed in the USA
CPSIA information can be obtained
at www.ICGtesting.com
LVHW070845141123
763833LV00021B/266